Deadliest Animals

Melissa Stewart

NATIONAL GEOGRAPHIC

Washington, D.C.

For Colin
—M.S.

Paperback ISBN: 978-1-4263-0757-7
Library Edition ISBN: 978-1-4263-0758-4

cover, Karine Aigner/ NationalGeographicStock.com; 1, Ian Waldie/ Getty Images; 2, Radius Images/ Getty Images; 4 (top), Gary Randall/ Taxi/ Getty Images; 4 (center), Duncan Noakes/ iStockphoto.com; 4 (bottom), James Martin/ The Image Bank/ Getty Images; 5, Stephen Robinson/ NHPA/ Photoshot; 6-7, Mitsuaki Iwago/ Minden Pictures; 8, Gerry Pearce/ Alamy; 9 (top), DEA/ Christian Ricci/ De Agostini/ Getty Images; 9 (bottom), SA team/ Foto Natura/ Minden Pictures/ NationalGeographicStock.com; 10, Ira Block/ NationalGeographicStock.com; 11, Rinie Van Meurs/ Minden Pictures; 13 (bottom), Jonathan & Angela Scott/ NHPA/ Photoshot; 13 (top), Jason Edwards/ NationalGeographicStock.com; 14, Beverly Joubert/ NationalGeographicStock.com; 15, Tim Fitzharris/ Minden Pictures/ NationalGeographicStock.com; 16-17, Karl Ammann/ Digital Vision/ Getty Images; 18, Konrad Wothe/ Minden Pictures/ NationalGeographicStock.com; 19, Frans Lanting/ NationalGeographicStock.com; 20, DLILLC/ Corbis; 21 (top), ohn Pitcher/ Design Pics/ Corbis; 21 (center), Radius Images/ Corbis; 21 (bottom), ack Goldfarb/ Design Pics// Corbis; 22, Bates Littlehales/ NationalGeographicStock.com; 23 (top), Deshakalyan Chowdhury/ AFP/ Getty Images; 23 (bottom), George Grall/ NationalGeographicStock.com; 24, Armin Maywald/ Foto Natura/ Minden Pictures/ NationalGeographicStock.com; 25 (top), Ho New/ Tasmania Police/ Reuters; 25 (bottom), Ian Waldie/ Getty Images; 26, Stephen Frink/ Science Faction/ Getty Images; 27, David Doubilet/ National Geographic/ Getty Images; 28, Cary Wolinsky/ NationalGeographicStock.com; 29, Michael Melford/ NationalGeographicStock.com; 30 (top left), Martin Harvey/ Gallo Images/ Getty Images; 30 (top right), Panoramic Images/ Getty Images; 30 (center left), Andrew Holt/ Photographer's Choice/ Getty Images; 30 (center right), Brian J. Skerry/ NationalGeographicStock.com; 30 (bottom left), Gary Vestal/ Riser/ Getty Images; 30 (bottom right), Paul Zahl/ NationalGeographicStock.com; 31 (top left), James Forte/ NationalGeographicStock.com; 31 (top right), Andrew Bannister/ Gallo Images/ Getty Images; 31 (center left), David B. Fleetham/ Photolibrary/ Getty Images; 31 (center right), Lius Angel Espinoza/ National Geographic My Shot; 31 (bottom), Heidi & Hans-Juergen Koch/ Minden Pictures/ Getty Images; 32-33, Gary Bell/ Taxi/ Getty Images; 33 (right), Viorika Prikhodko/ iStockphoto.com; 34 (left), Shane Drew/ iStockphoto.com; 34-35, Photographer/ NationalGeographicStock.com; 35 (inset), Hal Beral VWPics/ SuperStock; 36, Mark Moffett/ Minden Pictures; 37 (top), ZSSD/ Minden Pictures/ NationalGeographicStock.com; 37 (center), Mark Moffett/ Minden Pictures/ NationalGeographicStock.com; 37 (bottom), Mark Moffett/ Minden Pictures/ Getty Images; 38, Scott Leslie/ Minden Pictures/ NationalGeographicStock.com; 39, Zheng Jiayu/ XinHua/ Xinhua Press/ Corbis; 40, IMAGEMORE Co, Ltd./ Getty Images; 41, Mark Moffett/ Minden Pictures/ Getty Images; 42, David Maitland/ NHPA/ Photoshot; 43, Ian Waldie/ Getty Images; 44, David Scharf/ Science Faction/ Getty Images; 45, Mitsuhiko Imamori/ Minden Pictures/ NationalGeographicStock.com; 46 (bottom left), Keren Su/ The Image Bank/ Getty Images; 46, Armin Maywald/ Foto Naturs/ Minden Pictures/ NationalGeographicStock.com; 46 (center right), David Doubilet/ National Geographic/ Getty Images; 46 (top right), Karen Mower/ iStockphoto.com; 46 (bottom right), Ira Block/ NationalGeographicStock.com; 46 (top left), Gary Bell/ Taxi/ Getty Images; 47 (center right), Mark Moffett/ Minden Pictures/ Getty Images; 47 (bottom right), Deshakalyan Chowdhury/ AFP/ Getty Images; 47 (top right), Johan Swanepoel/ iStockphoto.com; 47 (center left), ZSSD/ Minden Pictures/ NationalGeographicStock.com; 47 (bottom left), Scott Leslie/ Minden Pictures/ NationalGeographicStock.com

Printed in the U.S.A.
10 /WOR/1

Table of Contents

Deadly Surprises

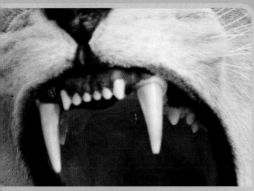

Huge teeth?
Check.

Razor-sharp claws?
Check.

Fast and fierce?
Check.

The African lion has all the features you'd expect to find in one of the world's deadliest animals. These powerful predators are skillful stalkers that usually hunt together in groups called "prides" and can take down prey ten times their size. That's why people often call lions "the kings of the jungle."

But are lions the deadliest
animals of all?

Not quite.

Lions certainly score high on the deadliest list, but they don't take the number one spot. And if you think all of Earth's most dangerous creatures are big, fierce hunters, you're in for some surprises.

Surprise 1:

Some deadly animals eat only plants.

Red kangaroos spend their days quietly nibbling on grasses, but when they feel threatened, watch out! A hard kick in the chest can break a person's ribs and collapse the lungs.

Surprise 2:

Some deadly animals are smaller than the palm of your hand.

Oak processionary (sounds like PRO-seh-shen-ary) caterpillars are only 2 inches long, but beware of their hairy bristles. They can cause rashes, asthma attacks, and even deadly allergic reactions.

DEADLY DEFINITIONS

ALLERGIC: When the body responds to something with a rash, breathing trouble, or even death

VENOM: A poisonous liquid inside some animals' bodies

Surprise 3:

Some deadly animals may be closer than you think.

Rattlesnakes live throughout the United States, and they bite about 8,000 people each year. Even though rattlesnake venom is deadly, most people get treated quickly and survive.

Saltwater Crocodiles

Saltwater crocodiles are just as fierce as polar bears—and just as patient, too.

Lurking below the water's surface, a croc lies in wait for its prey. When an unsuspecting animal passes by, the 1,000-pound beast explodes out of the water, grabs its victim, and drags it under the water to drown. Yikes!

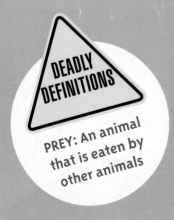

DEADLY DEFINITIONS

PREY: An animal that is eaten by other animals

⚠ **Crocodile Safety**

DANGER

Crocodiles inhabit this area.
Attacks cause injury or death.

– Keep away from the water's edge.
– Do not enter the water.

– Do not clean fish near the water's edge.
– Remove all fish and food waste.

The saltwater crocodile is the most deadly large predator. It can easily take down a water buffalo and has even been known to kill sharks off the coast of Australia.

Big and Brutal

Hippopotamuses

Hippopotamuses are usually gentle giants. During the day, they lounge and snooze in shallow water holes. At night, they lumber onto land and munch on grasses and leaves.

But if a boat gets between a hippo and the deep water or between a mother and her calf, the animal will panic. It may tip over the boat and attack the passengers with its powerful jaws.

weird but true

A hippo can outrun you on land and outswim you in the water. You don't stand a chance against an angry hippo!

Elephants

Like hippos, elephants are usually calm, peaceful animals. But when an elephant feels threatened, it will attack.

The huge herbivore can stab enemies with its tusks and crush them with its feet. Sometimes it grabs an attacker with its trunk and tosses the possible threat into the air.

Elephants are the largest animals on land, so they can do a lot of damage.

DEADLY DEFINITIONS

HERBIVORE: An animal that eats plants

Cape Buffaloes

Large herds of Cape buffaloes graze hour after hour on thick grasses. It might seem like they're focusing on their food, but they're also on the lookout for danger.

Death Toll

In Africa, Cape buffaloes are known as "black death" due to their dark color and ferocious nature.

When these huge, hulking animals feel angry or scared, they charge at enemies with their heads down. Often they charge together as a group. A stampede of Cape buffaloes can kill predators quickly with their sharp hooves and hooked horns.

Scary Snakes

About 3,000 species of snakes live on Earth, and most of them make venom. Snakes use venom to kill prey and protect themselves from enemies.

DEADLY DEFINITIONS

SPECIES: A group of similar creatures that can mate and produce healthy young

TOXIC: Poisonous, capable of causing injury or death

Most snakes are too small or too shy to attack humans. But about 300 species can kill a person who's in the wrong place at the wrong time.

Golden Eyelash Viper

Green Pit Viper

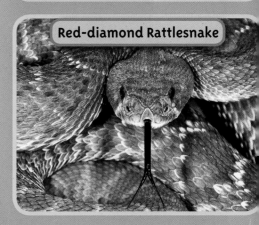

Red-diamond Rattlesnake

Toxic Tidbit

The Indian cobra's venom isn't as toxic as the venom of some other snakes, but it often lives close to people and that makes it a major threat. Indian cobra bites kill thousands of people each year in Asia.

21

Which snake is the deadliest of all?

That's a hard question to answer.

Hook-nosed Sea Snake

This fish-hunting reptile lives in coastal waters and has the most poisonous venom of any snake. Just one drop can kill a person. Like other snakes, it has lungs and breathes air, but it can stay underwater for up to five hours.

Russell's Viper

This snake lives in rice paddies and grassy areas of Asia and may bite farmers. Its venom isn't quite as toxic as the hook-nosed sea snake's venom, but it has more toxin in its body. That means it delivers more venom in each bite.

Black Mamba

Other snakes may have stronger venom, but the black mamba moves fast and isn't afraid to attack. When an enemy gets too close, the black mamba raises its head high and hisses. If the predator doesn't back off, the snake strikes again and again.

Ferocious Fish

Great White Shark

The great white shark is the largest meat-eating fish in the ocean. The sight of its huge mouth and 3,000 jagged teeth would send shivers up anyone's spine.

What makes this shark so dangerous? Its super senses. It hears well and has excellent eyesight. Most important, its sense of smell is 10,000 times better than ours.

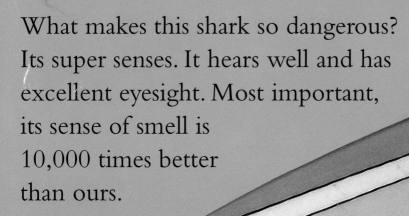

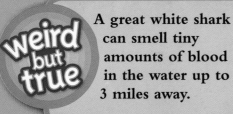

weird but true

A great white shark can smell tiny amounts of blood in the water up to 3 miles away.

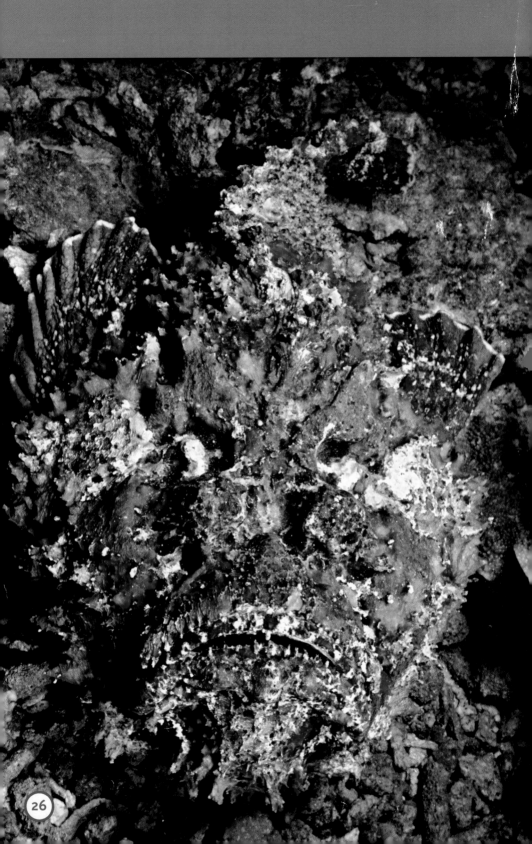

Stonefish

Stonefish are masters of disguise. Instead of swimming in search of food, they blend into their rocky surroundings and wait for prey to pass by.

DEADLY DEFINITIONS

PARALYZED: Unable to move

If a hungry predator grabs a stonefish— or a person accidentally steps on one— thirteen spiky spines deliver a painful blast of venom. The wound swells, the victim's muscles feel weak, and the area becomes paralyzed. If the person isn't treated, he or she could die.

Puffer Fish

When an enemy attacks, a puffer fish gulps water and blows up like a prickly balloon. But that's not the fish's only trick for protection.

If a predator manages to take a bite of a puffer fish, it gets a mouthful of nasty-tasting toxin. Yuck!

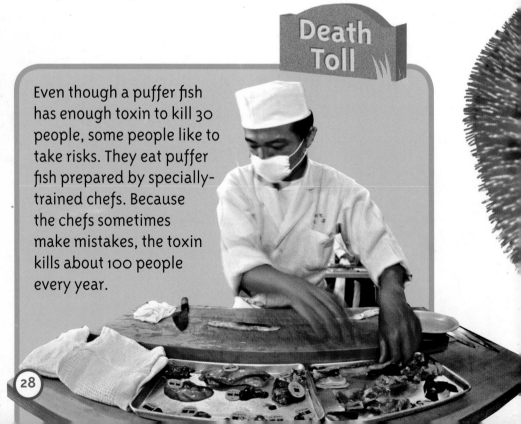

Death Toll

Even though a puffer fish has enough toxin to kill 30 people, some people like to take risks. They eat puffer fish prepared by specially-trained chefs. Because the chefs sometimes make mistakes, the toxin kills about 100 people every year.

10 Cool Things About Deadly Animals

1 Female lions do most of the hunting, but male lions always eat first.

2 On hot, sunny days, a crocodile pants like a dog to stay cool.

3 Most young fish are called fingerlings, but young sharks are called pups.

4 Baby hippopotamuses are born underwater.

5 If you shine a black light on a scorpion, it glows in the dark.

6 A jellyfish doesn't have a brain.

7 All snakes have teeth, but only snakes that make venom have fangs.

8 If an octopus loses an arm, another one will grow in its place.

9 Some poison dart frogs contain enough toxin to kill ten people.

10 A honeybee has five eyes—three small ones on top of its head and two large ones in front.

No Bones About It

Fish aren't the only sea creatures that can be hazardous to your health. Some ocean invertebrates can be just as deadly.

Box Jellyfish

You may have been stung by a jellyfish, but the box jellyfish is in a class by itself.

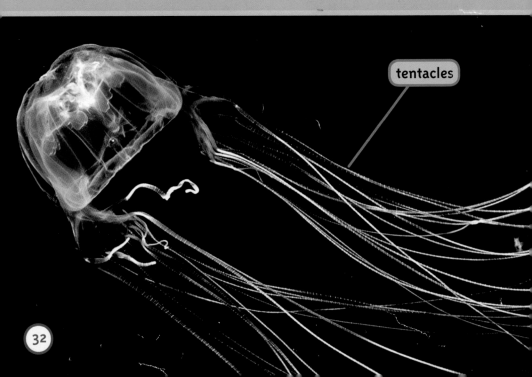

tentacles

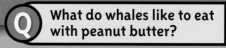

Toxic Tidbit

A box jellyfish's body is the size of a basketball, but its tentacles can be up to 9 feet long.

Each of its tentacles has thousands of tiny stinging cells. Together, they pack enough toxins to kill 60 people, and death can come in just 4 minutes.

body

tentacles

DEADLY DEFINITIONS

INVERTEBRATE: An animal with no backbone

33

Blue-ringed Octopus

A blue-ringed octopus is the size of a golf ball, but it has a deadly bite.

Most of the time, the octopus uses its toxic saliva to catch crabs and shrimp. But its powerful poison can paralyze up to twenty people. Within minutes, anything that attacks this little octopus stops breathing and dies.

DANGER

BLUE RING OCTOPUS

A blue-ringed octopus's skin is usually yellowish brown. But bright-blue spots or rings suddenly appear when the octopus feels scared.

Small But Deadly

The ocean isn't the only place on Earth with small, deadly creatures. They also live in fields and forests, wetlands and deserts.

Poison Dart Frogs

Scientists think that poison dart frogs eat toxic insects that make them deadly. Touch the slimy skin of these brightly-colored creatures and you could be dead in minutes.

☠ Toxic Tidbit

Some native rain forest peoples catch poison dart frogs, collect their venom, and rub it on darts they use to hunt. That's how the frogs got their name.

Honeybees

Honeybees help us by pollinating many of our favorite fruits, vegetables, and nuts. But they can also be deadly.

About 1 in 4,000 people is severely allergic to bee venom and can die after just one sting if left untreated. But all the toxin from a stinging swarm of angry bees can kill anyone.

DEADLY DEFINITIONS

POLLINATE: To transfer pollen from one flower to another, allowing plants to make fruit and seeds

What happened when the honeybee called its hive?

A It got a buzzy signal.

weird but true

Bee bearding is the practice of attracting bees to the human body by hanging the queen from the chin.

Scorpions

A scorpion's huge, claw-like pincers are its weapon of choice. But if a predator attacks or its prey puts up a fight … ZAP! A swift strike with the stinger on its tail usually does the trick.

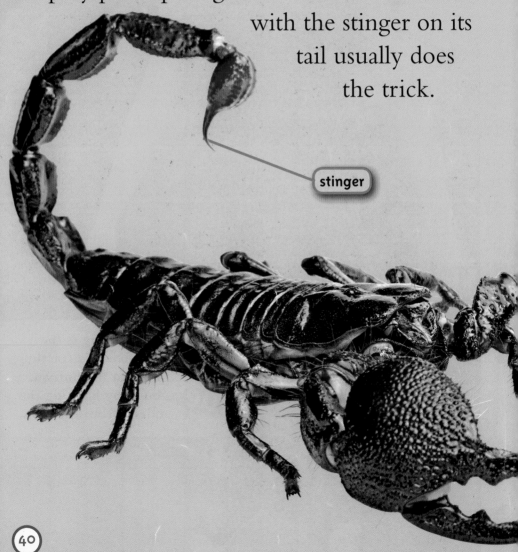

stinger

The stinger contains a hollow tube connected to two sacs full of venom. The scorpion controls the amount of venom its stinger delivers, so bigger victims get a bigger dose.

Death Toll

Of the nearly 2,000 scorpion species alive today, only 30 or 40 have venom strong enough to kill humans. Still, thousands of people die each year from scorpion stings.

Sydney Funnel Web Spider

Small and shiny. Dark and deadly. That's how people in Australia describe the Sydney funnel web spider.

Most of the time, this spider uses its sharp fangs and deadly venom to catch insects and other prey. But if a person gets too close, the spider won't hesitate to bite.

| Q | Why do spiders spin webs? | They don't know how to knit. | A |

☠ Toxic Tidbit

Scientists developed medicine to protect people from Sydney funnel web spider venom in 1981. No one has died from its bite since.

Deadliest of All

So what's the deadliest animal of all?

The mosquito—that pesky little insect with the whiny hum!

Mosquitoes carry some of the worst diseases on Earth, including malaria and West Nile virus. And

when a mosquito sucks blood from an animal, germs can enter the victim's body. That's why it's a good idea to use bug spray when there are insects around.

From tiny mosquitoes to gigantic elephants, the world's deadliest animals come in all sizes and shapes. And they live in every habitat you can think of. But each of them has a special way of keeping themselves safe in a dangerous world.

Glossary

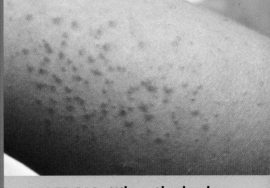

ALLERGIC: When the body responds to something with a rash, breathing trouble, or even death

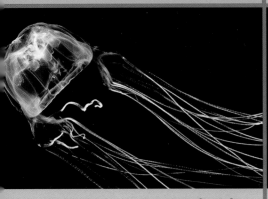

INVERTEBRATE: An animal with no backbone

PARALYZED: Unable to move

PREDATOR: An animal that hunts and eats other animals

SPECIES: A group of similar creatures that can mate and produce healthy young

CARNIVORE: An animal that eats the meat of other animals

HERBIVORE: An animal that eats plants

POLLINATE: To transfer pollen from one flower to another, allowing plants to make fruit and seeds

PREY: An animal that is eaten by other animals

TOXIC: Poisonous, capable of causing injury or death. A toxic substance is called a toxin.

VENOM: A poisonous liquid inside some animals' bodies

Index